IGNATZ

Also by Monica Youn:

Barter

IGNATZ

Monica Youn

Four Way Books
Tribeca

Please direct all inquiries to:
Editorial Office
Four Way Books
POB 535, Village Station
New York, NY 10014
www.fourwaybooks.com

Library of Congress Cataloging-in-Publication Data

Youn, Monica.
Ignatz / Monica Youn.
p. cm. — (A Stahlecker series selection)
ISBN 978-1-935536-01-7 (pbk. : alk. paper)
I. Title.
PS3625.O76I38 2010
811'.6--dc22
2009029463
3rd printing, 2021

This book is manufactured in the United States of America
and printed on acid-free paper.

Four Way Books is a not-for-profit literary press.
We are grateful for the assistance we receive from individual donors, public arts agencies, and private foundations.

This publication is made possible with public funds
from the National Endowment for the Arts
and from the New York State Council on the Arts, a state agency.

Distributed by University Press of New England
One Court Street, Lebanon, NH 03766

We are a proud member of the Council of Literary Magazines and Presses.

NATIONAL
ENDOWMENT
FOR THE ARTS
A great nation
deserves great art

State of the Arts

NYSCA

[clmp]

TABLE OF CONTENTS

As if my life were shaven
And fitted to a frame

—Emily Dickinson

I

O Ignatz won't you meet me
                by the blue bean bush?
Robed in the loveliest
                robe of the year.

Five ripe dewberries
                on a sweetgum leaf.
A dark red loveknot
                in my short black hair.

IGNATZ INVOKED

A gauze bandage wraps the land
and is unwound, stained orange with sulfates.

A series of slaps molds a mountain,
a fear uncoils itself, testing its long

cool limbs. A passing cloud
seizes up like a carburetor

and falls to earth, lies broken-
backed and lidless in the scree.

Acetylene torches now snug
in their holsters, shop-vacs

trundled back behind the dawn.
A mist becomes a murmur, becomes

a moan deepening the dust-
choked fissures in the rock *O pity us*

Ignatz O come to us by moonlight
O arch your speckled body over the earth.

IGNATZ AUBADE

Star-maps of broken capillaries:

crown of infrared
song of drifting dune

The smooth-boled trees of his interior
blossoming and unblossoming:

"I spent six days almost touching you."

LANDSCAPE WITH IGNATZ

The rawhide thighs of the canyon straddling the knobbled blue spine of the sky.

The bone-spurred heels of the canyon prodding the gaunt blue ribs of the sky.

The sunburnt mouth of the canyon biting the swollen blue tongue of the sky.

The hangnailed fingers of the canyon snagging the tangled blue hair of the sky.

The blistered thumbs of the canyon tracing the blue-veined throat of the sky.

The sleep-crusted lids of the canyon blink open . . . *your soft, your cerulean eye.*

IGNATZ IN AUGUST

you arch
up off me

sweat flowers
white out

of my every
desert pore

LETTER TO IGNATZ

O my dear devoir
O my dour devour

*

Your name:
                    an arrow
with a rope attached

could pull
                    this raft
across this river.

*

O bring me
my ordinary:

my trays

of soot
and sand

*

For tonight I am a window
in a cottage by the sea.

*

O mia paloma blanca
O my desert dune

my dove,

who now will
sing the praises

of a natural love?

IGNATZ OASIS

When you have left me
the sky drains of color

like the skin
of a tightening fist.

The sun commences
its gold prowl

batting at tinsel streamers
on the electric fan.

Crouching I hide
in the coolness I stole

from the brass rods
of your bed.

THE WEDDING OF IGNATZ

Weight
is the end

of wanting.

The simples
gleaming

in their rests.

In the game called
hypothesis

an orange

is gripped between
the chin

and shoulder

then is transferred
with care

and laughing

to the chin
and shoulder of

the next-in-line. Then

a flaming log
is rolled

into the river.

Then a chalk circle
is drawn

around each plate.

*

One day I walked
to the window

robed in the loveliest
robe of the year.

One day I knelt down
by the fountain.

A crown of parsley
a crown of dill.

One day my hands
closed on the handles.

A match tip was placed
beneath my tongue.

"Listen to me—someone
has tricked you.

There was never an apple."

THE DEATH OF IGNATZ

Fallow lies Ignatz,
his salt hands

helpless
wicking

moisture from the air.

II

O Ignatz won't you play me
    like a filigree flute?
I'd trill any tune it might
    please you to hear.

"O Sweet Adeline,"
    "Au clair de la lune,"
Your song my only voice,
    your breath my only air.

THE LABORS OF IGNATZ

[1]

your lionskin
overcoat

lined in lead

with barbed-wire
boutonniere

[2]

a decimated daisy:

H. L.'s M.*
H. L.'s M. N.**

---

* He loves me.
** He loves me not.

[3]

"fainting I follow . . ."

your name

picked out in rhinestones

on a red
silk leash

[4]

in surfeit
you wallow

in the pit

of your sufficiency

[5]

besmirched

you bathe
in a basin of moonlight:

a raft of toxins

    floats free

[6]

chain-stitches
of sparrow-song

    crudely suture

the tattered sunrise

[7]

soothe the waves

    with milk
    o my love

let cream rise richly

    to the surface
    of the sea

[8]

head bowed

    in acquiescence:
    metallic

pressure on the tongue

[9]

the belt
of your bathrobe

forlorn
on the floor

[10]

you grin:
a gloaty giant

thumbing his box of bits

[11]

the constellations
a tenement of ex-lovers

blotted out

by your sweat-
slick shoulders

[12]

There was something
 in his plea . . .

something that touched me.

AFTERWARDS IGNATZ

rose and without taking his leave of them opened the sliding glass door and vanished onto that lightless beach. And there were those who later said that he never opened that door, that the molecules of glass parted at his touch, or still others that he stepped through the glass door as some of his brothers might move swiftly through a downpour while never being wetted, for as his brothers were to the common run of men, so it is said that Ignatz was to his brothers. But the truth of it was that Ignatz slid open the door, stepped through, and slid it shut again so smoothly and swiftly that to distinguish one action from the other would be to count the blades of a flying helicopter, and that good door, well-greased in its gasket, did not betray him by a single ill-timed creak, so that by the time that they saw that he had gone from them, his dark head was already lost in the black waves of sand and the black waves of water. And even then, there were those who would have gone after him and had risen from their seats with brave and defiant words, but they were stayed by the wise counsel of others who admonished them that it would be as well to tether a missile with a filament of spiderweb as to dissuade Ignatz with their pleading from his chosen itinerary.

IGNATZ PACIFICUS

Travelling backwards on the Amtrak Surfliner,
Ignatz is firelord of the Pacific, CEO

of the thermal inversion, true husband
of the Santa Ana wind. Observe his hands,

sowers of wildfire, hovering over the wave-
embroidered armrests, see the tray table

fruitlessly offering up tidbits to his gaze.
Seven rainless months have sensitized the vast

reticulations of his concern, he is each black ash
that infiltrates each kitchen windowscreen,

he is each ember hissing its defiance
on the blue surface of a kidney-shaped pool.

trudges through the sand and up the cliff path leading, as he supposes, to the parking lot . . . only to find himself descending just as abruptly to another beach—the cliff no cliff in fact, but only a kind of curtain wall, taller than it is wide. Here, too, the babies, the lovers, the paint-by-numbers pattern of ice plants and purple mosses on the dunes. The waves backlit at this time of day, of a green so transparent he can clearly make out the slim bulb-headed waterweeds within them, pulled upright—as if on leashes—as each wave reaches its cresting point, then bowing down, an obeisance of froth and clicking pebbles. To the left, and farther out, black chess pawns signifying surfers stretch out a line to the horizon—waiting, bobbing and waiting—a sight that Ignatz finds to be unexpectedly nerve-wracking, a background music tape loop *'tis a gift to be simple / 'tis a gift to be free*

I-40 IGNATZ

The tanker
trucks so

gaily caparisoned:

rows of red and
yellow lights,

o night

of joy
and blitz.

A cop car drowses
in the scrub

cottonwoods. Utmost.

Utmosted. There is
a happy land.

Far, far.

The bleaching fields.
The silica-coated trees.

Some plain

browns. The girl
at the CITGO

station says *Don't
you come here*

all the time?

ERSATZ IGNATZ

The clockwork saguaros sprout extra faces like planaria stroked by
a razor. *Chug*

say the sparrows, emitting fluffs of steam. *Chug chug* say the piston-powered
ground squirrels.

The tumbleweeds circle on retrofitted tracks, but the blue pasteboard welkin
is much dented by little winds.

The yuccas pulse softly under the grow-light sconces.

Here is the door he will paint on the rock.

Here is the glass floor of the cliff.

He'll enter from the west, backlit in orange isinglass, pyrite
pendants glinting from the fringes of his voice.

SEMPER IGNATZ

How could it have been other

than abrupt
when as ever

in medias Ignatz remarked,

Sometimes   I don't   like

fucking.   Whoosh!   A billow

of white cambric sheets the scene,
through which her nipples glow dully,

taillights   in snow.

IGNATZ AT THE SHRINE OF THE SINNERS

Night like a black

glass bell
and the fading

echo of the detox
mantras:

helpless   helpless
helpless   helpless

if fleshly importuning
were to fall silent . . .

*

Each sinner's left behind

a little sinner
diorama:

laminated photos,
silk flowers

strung with wire.
Ignatz

tiptoes unseen through
thickets

of votive prayer
candles

holding as his candle
snuffer

an aluminum
rose.

[AND THE CHORUS KICKS IN]

Ignatz!
he's a stalker

or a snigger or
a stain the v

on his forehead
stands for villain

or for vain o
tongueless talker

will you never teach him shame?

THE DEATH OF IGNATZ

The mesas
sink to their knees

and let the snickering dunes
crawl over them.

III

O Ignatz won't you dress me
            in your leadlined coat,
Proof against passion
            resistant to tears,

I'll stroll through the streets
            with a safeguarded strut,
Set up shop in the kissing booth—
            Buyer beware.

AT THE FREE CLINIC IGNATZ

snoozes with his head down on the secondhand classroom desk with his elbow on the part of it that curves around to support his elbow so that he can shut his eyes against the bend of his own arm with his cheek pressed against the laminated desktop and his fingers just draping over the laminated plywood edge that is the same edge that curves around to dig slightly into his ribcage which is tilted so his lower spine stays in contact with the molded contours of the glossy seagreen chair that curves around to where his thighs begin and rises slightly where his legs need to rise and rounds off gently and ends just where his legs need to bend down to the floor so that if this is a lesson in how something harder and something softer can achieve a mutuality if the harder thing has a curvature that suggests an accommodating mindset and the softer thing is willing to relinquish some measure of contingency so the softer thing can come temporarily to rest and if a test were devised on the subject of this lesson then what would be gained for one who took this test and passed it or one who took this test and failed?

IGNATZ IN FURS

Her head
reared back

in an animal
posture—

Ignatz
as always

obliged.

       *

Miss May   more modest
still in her   stockings

       *

Ignatz thought again of

   "the wild carnation,"

of the equable nature
his friend had described

   that rainy night.

*

Question: What is it that you're testing?

Question: Is there a white spot at which you will bend?

IGNATZ PURSUER

her nostrils straining to the limits
of their stretch and her lips glued shut

and her fingers clamped over her mouth
for good measure she is running

running from Ignatz and the night
like a drumskin and her heart like someone

locked in the trunk of a car and if there were
only time god she would spit it out

into her palm she would pry out the mortar
between two bricks and wedge it in there

she would bury it under the succulents
in the municipal planter she would catch

a piebald pigeon and tie it to its foot but
there is no time and she cannot bring herself

to swallow it and he is coming up fast
behind her taking lampposts in his stride

ON IGNATZ'S EYEBROW

the way water is always rushing between a ferry

and its dock in that ever-present gap where

the rush is the speed of the water and the rush

is the sound of the water and the water is

bitterly cold and is foul in its bitterness and

the gap is irreducible space and time and

is the ache felt by the ferry in the cold

of its iron bones which will never clang

against the framework of the dock

in the satisfying clash of solid surfaces because

the gap is where such satisfaction helplessly

dissolves the way Ignatz now feels his anger

dissipating in that self-same gap between

the trigger and the smack between his anger

and its object the way one eyebrow

can never meet the other in a true unbroken v

no matter how doomy how dour

how darksome his invariable frown.

THE SUBJECT IGNATZ

Once more an urge; once more a succumb.

Even as a lawn
or tree

is more attractive
when configured

as individual
leaves

than as
a seamless

green
integument.

        *

Asbestos
interlude:

the rubber
button

replumps itself.

        *

The pin
pokes through

the black
wax

and scratches
the bottom

of the pan.

*

All the unseen
valves

of the night
click open,

a blue-violet
pour down

a fretless throat.

*

There can be no
launch, only

trajectory

in this elastic
room.

X AS A FUNCTION OF DISTANCE FROM IGNATZ

(she opens the door)
(he is twelve inches
away) her fingers

still splayed across the
battened-down brass latch
of his sternum (she

closes the door) (he
is eight feet away)
her palm skids down the

banister clings to
the fluted globe of
the finial (he

is twenty-eight feet
away) (she opens
the door) the black air

is fast flowing and
cold (she closes the
door) she clutches her

thin intimacy
tight under her chin
and trips down the steps

(he is forty feet
away) the stiff wind
palpably stripping

his scent from her hair
from the numb fingers
she raises to her

mouth a cab pulls up
(she opens the door)
she bends the body

hitherto upright
(she closes the door)
the cracked brown vinyl

(he is ninety feet
away) biting the
backs of her thighs red

blotches suffusing
her cheeks I'm sorry
please stop she says (he

is four hundred feet
away) please stop the
cab (she opens the

door) the cab stops she
pushes a twenty
through the slot (he is

seven hundred feet
away) (she closes
the door) the husk of

something dry and light
falls to the sidewalk
crumbles away (she

opens the door) (he
is two feet away)
(she closes the door)

IGNATZ AT THE _____ HOTEL

Five smudged lines on her cheek:

> soot on the blue-sprigged pillowcase,
> keyholes sealed with wax.

A moth sobbed brokenly in the middle of the room.

> A drop of pleasure
> shimmied down his spine.

His bluenailed fingers fled into her mouth.

THE DEATH OF IGNATZ

scratched in the plexi
of the defunct

jukebox—*god*
I was such

a simple
song

IV

O Ignatz won't you flee
        into the whitherwander woods?
Cower in a covert
        until the coast is clear?

A silverleafed bower
        of shivering shade:
I will weave you a shelter
        of my living hair.

IGNATZ DOMESTICUS

Then one day she noticed the forest had begun to bleed into her waking life.

There were curved metal plates on the trees to see around corners.

She thought to brush her hand against his thigh.

She thought to trace the seam of his jeans with her thumbnail.

The supersaturated blues were beginning to pixillate around the edges, to become a kind of grammar.

She placed a saucer of water under her lamp and counted mosquitoes as they drowned.

Soot amassed in drifts in the corners of the room.

She pressed her thumb into the hollow of his throat for a while and then let him go.

SO SWEETLY SLUMBERS IGNATZ IN HIS SYLVAN BOWER

je te cacherai et je te garderai

bivouac

      a leaf-
      hammock

long leaves of daylilies   knotted into a mat

      breeze breeze
      a dappling breeze

        sunlight

          pitterpatter

              the silver birch trees

a canopy so cunningly wrought

        of cobwebs
        of creeping fig

but there   a black blot   against a green
                                              a green bough

        a policeman's glove

        by a spiraling
                tendril suspended

so that an insolent sunbeam does not strike upon the silver cheek

        of Ignatz no does not

shine like glass

A THEORY OF IGNATZ

To say that Ignatz floats at the level of the neighbor is really to assert his status as denominator; *i.e.*, he is a plane tilted at the *ecliptic*, both in its sense of inclination at an angle of 23 degrees, 27 minutes, and also in its palimpsestic sense, with a scrim of the Latin root *ecliptica* (line) coyly veiling the Greek *ekleiptikos* (to fail to appear).

SPRINGES TO CATCH IGNATZ

Corrugations, leaf-litter,
a palm-sized blaze.

The leer of each boulder,

each mask
of white lichen.

The lopped branches

of the pines black
and reaching,

and the woods softly clicking,

crowded
with fringed holes.

The light shifts over

one notch
to the mangy reds,

the attenuated

greens of day-
for-night. Then

a necklace

of beer bottles snagged
on a stump, then

five aspen leaves

skewered on five
living ash twigs.

IGNATZ INCARCERATED

suddenly	separate	mirrors
six	story	cellblock
Ignatz	entrance	squadron
paper	planes	snow
squaws	promise	war

IGNATZ RECIDIVIST

to blush
to blame
to bleed
to bless

helpless
helpless
helplessness

INVISIBLE IGNATZ

I would forget you were it not that unseen flutes
keep whistling the curving phrases of your body.

WINGED IGNATZ

There are twenty-seven feathers.

There are fifteen
feathers on the right

shoulder blade, twelve on the left—

curving outwards,
then streaming

down the back. When I say

"feathers," I mean to say
lines. Undulating lines,

more like hair than like feathers,

since, unlike feathers,
these lines do not convey

a ruched or corrugated effect

as might be rendered
by layered tiers of scallops,

or by a fingered edge. Instead of "lines"

I might more precisely
have said "cuts"—

discontinuous cuts, dotted with blood clots.

Flinches cluster
at the clots

like mayflies, as one imagines the blade

snagging in the skin,
where the cuts

cross one another. Mayflies, too,
are winged, but
no one wants them,

unless to convey a sense

of the ephemeral: a fan
of surface scratches

that splay across the shoulders

but do not break
the skin—merely

exhortatory, inviting one to read

the underlying cuts as
dimensional, on the verge

of lifting out of the skin, unfurling

above the shoulders,
lines of blood

fleshing themselves, then

feathering themselves,
in strength and mass

rivaling the body, muscle-bound,

that submitted
to give them birth.

IGNATZ: POP QUIZ

Question 1:

A tetherball

          is swinging

in a horizontal circle

          around a pole

attached

          with a 2m long

massless rope.

Question 2:

"Tell me when you can feel this."

THE DEATH OF IGNATZ

The architect leapt

from the bright
bell tower

and the sea
slunk back

to her cage

NOTES

George Herriman's *Krazy Kat* comic strip was published in U.S. newspapers from 1913 to 1944. The strip is set in Coconino County, Arizona, and stars Krazy Kat, a feline of indeterminate gender and mutable patois. Krazy is hopelessly in love with Ignatz Mouse, a rodent of criminal tendencies, who, in turn, despises Krazy and whose greatest pleasure is to bean the lovelorn cat in the head with a brick. Krazy interprets these missiles as tokens of reciprocated affection, and the cat-mouse-brick-love cycle recurs in almost every strip. Ignatz's repeated assaults upon Krazy incur the righteous wrath of Officer Bull Pupp, the canine sheriff of Coconino County, who is sweet on Krazy and who takes every opportunity to spy out Ignatz's crimes and to drag the recidivist mouse off to jail.

"Landscape with Ignatz," "Letter to Ignatz," and "I-40 Ignatz" quote Krazy.

The first "Untitled (Krazy's Song)" and "The Wedding of Ignatz" quote the same phrase from Saint-John Perse's *Anabase*.

The poem "The Labors of Ignatz" is, of course, based on the Labors of Heracles, which are [1] the Nemean Lion; [2] the Lernean Hydra; [3] the Hind of Artemis; [4] the Erymanthian Boar; [5] the Augean Stables; [6] the Stymphalian Birds; [7] the Cretan Bull; [8] the Horses of Diomedes; [9] the Girdle of Hippolyta; [10] the Cattle of Geryon; [11] the Apples of the Hesperides; and [12] Cerberus. Section 2 of the poem quotes Krazy. Section 3 of the poem quotes Sir Thomas Wyatt's "Whoso list to hunt." Section 12 of the poem quotes Officer Pupp.

"Ignatz at the Shrine of the Sinners" quotes St. Augustine's *Confessions*.

The epigraph of "The Subject Ignatz" quotes Officer Pupp.

"X as a Function of Distance from Ignatz" owes a stylistic debt to Aaron Kunin's *Folding Ruler Star.*

"Ignatz in Furs" quotes *The Tale of Genji*.

"So Sweetly Slumbers Ignatz in his Sylvan Bower" includes an epigraph from *Les Parapluies de Cherbourg.*

"Winged Ignatz" is for Stephen Elliott.

ACKNOWLEDGMENTS

Thanks are due to the editors of the following publications, where some of these poems first appeared:

The Awl.com, The Brooklyn Rail, Columbia, Cue: A Journal of Prose Poetry, Fence, Guernica, Gulf Coast, The Paris Review, and *Tin House.*

Thanks to the Library of Congress Witter Bynner Fellowship, the Rockefeller Foundation / Bellagio, the MacDowell Colony, the Corporation of Yaddo, my parents, Whitney Armstrong, Drew Daniel, Martin Schmidt, Charles Simic, and especially to Stephen Burt, Katy Lederer, Ryan Murphy, Mark Wunderlich, and Jason Zuzga, who provided extensive help with this manuscript.

Monica Youn is an attorney at the Brennan Center for Justice at NYU
School of Law, where she is the Director of the Money in Politics project.
She has been awarded poetry fellowships from the Library of Congress, the
Rockefeller Foundation, and Stanford University, and has taught creative
writing at Pratt Institute and Columbia University.